M.1.25

THE DOORS OF
PERCEPTION

THE DOORS OF PERCEPTION

Aldous Huxley

PERENNIAL LIBRARY
Harper & Row, Publishers
New York

THE DOORS OF PERCEPTION

Copyright 1954 by Aldous Huxley.

Printed in the United States of America.

First PERENNIAL LIBRARY edition published 1970 by Harper & Row, Publishers, Inc.

Library of Congress catalog card number: 54-5833.

"If the doors of perception were cleansed every thing would appear to man as it is, infinite."

WILLIAM BLAKE

For M

THE DOORS OF
PERCEPTION

It was in 1886 that the German pharmacologist, Louis Lewin, published the first systematic study of the cactus, to which his own name was subsequently given. *Anhalonium Lewinii* was new to science. To primitive religion and the Indians of Mexico and the American Southwest it was a friend of immemorially long standing. Indeed, it was much more than a friend. In the words of one of the early Spanish visitors to the New World, "they eat a root which they call peyote, and which they venerate as though it were a deity."

Why they should have venerated it as a deity became apparent when such eminent psychologists as Jaensch, Havelock Ellis and Weir Mitchell began their experiments with mescalin, the active principle of peyote. True, they stopped short at a point well this side of idolatry; but all concurred in assigning to mescalin a position among drugs of unique distinction. Administered in suitable doses, it changes the quality of consciousness more profoundly and yet is less toxic than any other substance in the pharmacologist's repertory.

Mescalin research has been going on sporadically ever since the days of Lewin and Havelock Ellis. Chemists have not merely isolated the alkaloid; they have learned how to synthesize it, so that the supply no longer depends on the sparse and intermittent crop of a desert cactus. Alienists have dosed themselves with mescalin in the hope thereby of coming to a better, a first-hand, understanding of their patients' mental processes. Working unfortunately upon too few subjects within too narrow a range of circumstances, psychologists have observed and catalogued some of the drug's more striking effects. Neurologists and physiologists have found out something about the mechanism of its action upon the central nervous system. And at least one professional philosopher has taken mescalin for the light it may throw on such ancient, unsolved riddles as the place of mind in nature and the relationship between brain and consciousness.

There matters rested until, two or three years ago, a new and perhaps highly significant fact was observed.*

* See the following papers: "Schizophrenia. A New Approach." By Humphry Osmond and John Smythies. *Journal of Mental Science.* Vol. XCVIII. April, 1952.

"On Being Mad." By Humphry Osmond. *Saskatchewan Psychiatric Services Journal.* Vol. I. No. 2. September, 1952.

Actually the fact had been staring everyone in the face for several decades; but nobody, as it happened, had noticed it until a young English psychiatrist, at present working in Canada, was struck by the close similarity, in chemical composition, between mescalin and adrenalin. Further research revealed that lysergic acid, an extremely potent hallucinogen derived from ergot, has a structural biochemical relationship to the others. Then came the discovery that adrenochrome, which is a product of the decomposition of adrenalin, can produce many of the symptoms observed in mescalin intoxication. But adrenochrome probably occurs spontaneously in the human body. In other words, each one of us may be capable of manufacturing a chemical, minute doses of which are known to cause profound changes in consciousness. Certain of these changes are similar to those which occur in that most characteristic plague of the twentieth century, schizophrenia. Is the mental disorder due to a chemical disorder? And is the chemical disorder due, in its turn, to psychological distresses affecting the

---

"The Mescalin Phenomena." By John Smythies. *The British Journal of the Philosophy of Science*. Vol. III. February, 1953.

"Schizophrenia: A New Approach." By Abram Hoffer, Humphry Osmond and John Smythies. *Journal of Mental Science*. Vol. C. No. 418. January, 1954.

Numerous other papers on the biochemistry, pharmacology, psychology and neurophysiology of schizophrenia and the mescalin phenomena are in preparation.

adrenals? It would be rash and premature to affirm it. The most we can say is that some kind of a *prima facie* case has been made out. Meanwhile the clue is being systematically followed, the sleuths—biochemists, psychiatrists, psychologists—are on the trail.

By a series of, for me, extremely fortunate circumstances I found myself, in the spring of 1953, squarely athwart that trail. One of the sleuths had come on business to California. In spite of seventy years of mescalin research, the psychological material at his disposal was still absurdly inadequate, and he was anxious to add to it. I was on the spot and willing, indeed eager, to be a guinea pig. Thus it came about that, one bright May morning, I swallowed four-tenths of a gram of mescalin dissolved in half a glass of water and sat down to wait for the results.

We live together, we act on, and react to, one another; but always and in all circumstances we are by ourselves. The martyrs go hand in hand into the arena; they are crucified alone. Embraced, the lovers desperately try to fuse their insulated ecstasies into a single self-transcendence; in vain. By its very nature every embodied spirit is doomed to suffer and enjoy in solitude. Sensations, feelings, insights, fancies—all these are private and, except through symbols and at second hand, incommunicable. We can pool information about experiences, but never the experiences themselves. From family to nation, every human group is a society of island universes.

Most island universes are sufficiently like one another to permit of inferential understanding or even of mutual empathy or "feeling into." Thus, remembering our own bereavements and humiliations, we can condole with others in analogous circumstances, can put ourselves (always, of course, in a slightly Pickwickian sense) in their places. But in certain cases communication between universes is incomplete or even nonexistent. The mind is its own place, and the places inhabited by the insane and the exceptionally gifted are so different from the places where ordinary men and women live, that there is little or no common ground of memory to serve as a basis for understanding or fellow feeling. Words are uttered, but fail to enlighten. The things and events to which the symbols refer belong to mutually exclusive realms of experience.

To see ourselves as others see us is a most salutary gift. Hardly less important is the capacity to see others as they see themselves. But what if these others belong to a different species and inhabit a radically alien universe? For example, how can the sane get to know what it actually feels like to be mad? Or, short of being born again as a visionary, a medium, or a musical genius, how can we ever visit the worlds which, to Blake, to Swedenborg, to Johann Sebastian Bach, were home? And how can a man at the extreme limits of ectomorphy and cerebrotonia ever put himself in the place of one at the limits of endomorphy and viscerotonia, or, except within certain circumscribed areas, share the feelings of one who stands at the limits of mesomorphy and somatotonia? To the unmitigated behaviorist such questions, I suppose, are meaningless. But for those who theoretically believe what in practice they know to be true—namely, that there is an inside to experience as well as an outside—the problems posed are real problems, all the more grave for being, some completely insoluble, some soluble only in exceptional circumstances and by methods not available to everyone. Thus, it seems virtually certain that I shall never know what it feels like to be Sir John Falstaff or Joe Louis. On the other hand, it had always seemed to me possible that, through hypnosis, for example, or autohypnosis, by means of systematic meditation, or else by taking the appropriate drug, I might so change my ordinary mode of consciousness as to be able to know, from the inside, what the visionary, the medium, even the mystic were talking about.

From what I had read of the mescalin experience I was convinced in advance that the drug would admit me, at least for a few hours, into the kind of inner world described by Blake and Æ. But what I had expected did not happen. I had expected to lie with my eyes shut, looking at visions of many-colored geometries, of animated architectures, rich with gems and fabulously lovely, of landscapes with heroic figures, of symbolic dramas trembling perpetually on the verge of the ultimate revelation. But I had not reckoned, it was evident, with the idiosyncrasies of my mental make-up, the facts of my temperament, training and habits.

I am and, for as long as I can remember, I have always been a poor visualizer. Words, even the pregnant words of poets, do not evoke pictures in my mind. No hypnagogic visions greet me on the verge of sleep. When I recall something, the memory does not present itself to me as a vividly seen event or object. By an effort of the will, I can evoke a not very vivid image of what happened yesterday afternoon, of how the Lungarno used to look before the bridges were destroyed, of the Bayswater Road when the only buses were green and tiny and drawn by aged horses at three and a half miles an hour. But such images have little substance and absolutely no autonomous life of their own. They stand to real, perceived objects in the same relation as Homer's ghosts stood to the men of flesh and blood, who came to visit them in the shades. Only when I have a high temperature do my mental images come to independent life. To those in whom the faculty of visualization is strong my inner world must seem curiously drab, limited and uninteresting. This was the world—a poor thing but my own—which I expected to see transformed into something completely unlike itself.

The change which actually took place in that world was in no sense revolutionary. Half an hour after swallowing the drug I became aware of a slow dance of golden lights. A little later there were sumptuous red surfaces swelling and expanding from bright nodes of energy that vibrated with a continuously changing, patterned life. At another time the closing of my eyes revealed a complex of gray structures, within which pale bluish spheres kept emerging into intense solidity and, having emerged, would slide noiselessly upwards, out of sight. But at no time were there faces or forms of men or animals. I saw no landscapes, no enormous spaces, no magical growth and metamorphosis of buildings, nothing remotely like a drama or a parable. The other world to which mescalin admitted me was not the world of visions; it existed out there, in what I could see with my eyes open. The great change was in the realm of objective fact. What had happened to my subjective universe was relatively unimportant.

I took my pill at eleven. An hour and a half later, I was sitting in my study, looking intently at a small glass vase. The vase contained only three flowers—a full-blown Belle of Portugal rose, shell pink with a hint at every petal's base of a hotter, flamier hue; a large magenta and cream-colored carnation; and, pale purple at the end of its broken stalk, the bold heraldic blossom of an iris. Fortuitous and provisional, the little nosegay broke all the rules of traditional good taste. At breakfast that morning I had been struck by the lively dissonance of its colors. But that was no longer the point. I was not looking now at an unusual flower arrangement. I was seeing what Adam had seen on the morning of his creation—the miracle, moment by moment, of naked existence.

"Is it agreeable?" somebody asked. (During this part of the experiment, all conversations were recorded on a dictating machine, and it has been possible for me to refresh my memory of what was said.)

"Neither agreeable nor disagreeable," I answered. "It just *is*."

Istigkeit—wasn't that the word Meister Eckhart liked to use? "Is-ness." The Being of Platonic philosophy—except that Plato seems to have made the enormous, the grotesque mistake of separating Being from becoming and identifying it with the mathematical abstraction of the Idea. He could never, poor fellow, have seen a bunch of flowers shining with their own inner light and all but quivering under the pressure of the significance with which they were charged; could never have perceived that what rose and iris and carnation so intensely signified was nothing more, and nothing less, than what they were—a transience that was yet eternal life, a perpetual perishing that was at the same time pure Being, a bundle of minute, unique particulars in which, by some unspeakable and yet self-evident paradox, was to be seen the divine source of all existence.

I continued to look at the flowers, and in their living light I seemed to detect the qualitative equivalent of breathing—but of a breathing without returns to a starting point, with no recurrent ebbs but only a repeated flow from beauty to heightened beauty, from deeper to ever deeper meaning. Words like "grace" and "transfiguration" came to my mind, and this, of course, was what, among other things, they stood for. My eyes traveled from the rose to the carnation, and from that feathery incandescence to the smooth scrolls of sentient amethyst which were the iris. The Beatific Vision, *Sat Chit Ananda*, Being-Awareness-Bliss—for the first time I understood, not on the verbal level, not by inchoate hints or at a distance, but precisely and completely what those prodigious syllables referred to. And then I remembered a passage I had read in one of Suzuki's essays. "What is the Dharma-Body of the Buddha?" ("The Dharma-Body of the Buddha" is another way of saying Mind, Suchness, the Void, the Godhead.) The question is asked in a Zen monastery by an earnest and bewildered novice. And with the prompt irrelevance of one of the Marx Brothers, the Master answers, "The hedge at the bottom of the garden." "And the man who realizes this truth," the novice dubiously inquires, "what, may I ask, is he?" Groucho gives him a whack over the shoulders with his staff and answers, "A golden-haired lion."

It had been, when I read it, only a vaguely pregnant piece of nonsense. Now it was all as clear as day, as evident as Euclid. Of course the Dharma-Body of the Buddha was the hedge at the bottom of the garden. At the same time, and no less obviously, it was these flowers, it was anything that I—or rather the blessed Not-I, released for a moment from my throttling embrace—cared to look at. The books, for example, with which my study walls were lined. Like the flowers, they glowed, when I looked at them, with brighter colors, a profounder significance. Red books, like rubies; emerald books; books bound in white jade; books of agate; of aquamarine, of yellow topaz; lapis lazuli books whose color was so intense, so intrinsically meaningful, that they seemed to be on the point of leaving the shelves to thrust themselves more insistently on my attention.

"What about spatial relationships?" the investigator inquired, as I was looking at the books.

It was difficult to answer. True, the perspective looked rather odd, and the walls of the room no longer seemed to meet in right angles. But these were not the really important facts. The really important facts were that spatial relationships had ceased to matter very much and that my mind was perceiving the world in terms of other than spatial categories. At ordinary times the eye concerns itself with such problems as *Where?—How far? —How situated in relation to what?* In the mescalin experience the implied questions to which the eye responds are of another order. Place and distance cease to be of much interest. The mind does its perceiving in terms of intensity of existence, profundity of significance, relationships within a pattern. I saw the books, but was not at all concerned with their positions in space. What I noticed, what impressed itself upon my mind was the fact that all of them glowed with living light and that in some the glory was more manifest than in others. In this context position and the three dimensions were beside the point. Not, of course, that the category of space had been abolished. When I got up and walked about, I could do so quite normally, without misjudging the whereabouts of objects. Space was still there; but it had lost its predominance. The mind was primarily concerned, not with measures and locations, but with being and meaning.

And along with indifference to space there went an even more complete indifference to time.

"There seems to be plenty of it," was all I would answer, when the investigator asked me to say what I felt about time.

Plenty of it, but exactly how much was entirely irrelevant. I could, of course, have looked at my watch; but my watch, I knew, was in another universe. My actual experience had been, was still, of an indefinite duration or alternatively of a perpetual present made up of one continually changing apocalypse.

From the books the investigator directed my attention to the furniture. A small typing table stood in the center of the room; beyond it, from my point of view, was a wicker chair and beyond that a desk. The three pieces formed an intricate pattern of horizontals, uprights and diagonals—a pattern all the more interesting for not being interpreted in terms of spatial relationships. Table, chair and desk came together in a composition that was like something by Braque or Juan Gris, a still life recognizably related to the objective world, but rendered without depth, without any attempt at photographic realism. I was looking at my furniture, not as the utilitarian who has to sit on chairs, to write at desks and tables, and not as the cameraman or scientific recorder, but as the pure aesthete whose concern is only with forms and their relationships within the field of vision or the picture space. But as I looked, this purely aesthetic, Cubist's-eye view gave place to what I can only describe as the sacramental vision of reality. I was back where I had been when I was looking at the flowers—back in a world where everything shone with the Inner Light, and was infinite in its significance. The legs, for example, of that chair—how miraculous their tubularity, how supernatural their polished smoothness! I spent several minutes—or was it several centuries?—not merely gazing at those bamboo legs, but actually *being* them—or rather being myself in them; or, to be still more accurate (for "I" was not involved in the case, nor in a certain sense were "they") being my Not-self in the Not-self which was the chair.

Reflecting on my experience, I find myself agreeing with the eminent Cambridge philosopher, Dr. C. D. Broad, "that we should do well to consider much more seriously than we have hitherto been inclined to do the type of theory which Bergson put forward in connection with memory and sense perception. The suggestion is that the function of the brain and nervous system and sense organs is in the main *eliminative* and not productive. Each person is at each moment capable of remembering all that has ever happened to him and of perceiving everything that is happening everywhere in the universe. The function of the brain and nervous system is to protect us from being overwhelmed and confused by this mass of largely useless and irrelevant knowledge, by shutting out most of what we should otherwise perceive or remember at any moment, and leaving only that very small and special selection which is likely to be practically useful." According to such a theory, each one of us is potentially Mind at Large. But in so far as we are animals, our business is at all costs to survive. To make biological survival possible, Mind at Large has to be funneled through the reducing valve of the brain and nervous system. What comes out at the other end is a measly trickle of the kind of consciousness which will help us to stay alive on the surface of this particular planet. To formulate and express the contents of this reduced awareness, man has invented and endlessly elaborated those symbol-systems and implicit philosophies which we call languages. Every individual is at once the beneficiary and the victim of the linguistic tradition into which he has been born—the beneficiary inasmuch as language gives access to the accumulated records of other people's experience, the victim in so far as it confirms him in the belief that reduced awareness is the only awareness and as it bedevils his sense of reality, so that he is all too apt to take his concepts for data, his words for actual things. That which, in the language of religion, is called "this world" is the universe of reduced awareness, expressed, and, as it were, petrified by language. The various "other worlds," with which human beings erratically make contact are so many elements in the totality of the awareness belonging to Mind at Large. Most people, most of the time, know only what comes through the reducing valve and is consecrated as genuinely real by the local language. Certain persons, however, seem to be born with a kind of by-pass that circumvents the reducing valve. In others temporary by-passes may be acquired either spontaneously, or as the result of deliberate "spiritual exercises," or through hypnosis, or by means of drugs. Through these permanent or temporary by-passes there flows, not indeed the perception "of everything that is happening everywhere in the universe" (for the by-pass does not abolish the reducing valve, which still excludes the total content of Mind at Large), but something more than, and above all something different from, the carefully selected utilitarian material which our narrowed, individual minds regard as a complete, or at least sufficient, picture of reality.

The brain is provided with a number of enzyme systems which serve to co-ordinate its workings. Some of these enzymes regulate the supply of glucose to the brain cells. Mescalin inhibits the production of these enzymes and thus lowers the amount of glucose available to an organ that is in constant need of sugar. When mescalin reduces the brain's normal ration of sugar what happens? Too few cases have been observed, and therefore a comprehensive answer cannot yet be given. But what happens to the majority of the few who have taken mescalin under supervision can be summarized as follows.

(1) The ability to remember and to "think straight" is little if at all reduced. (Listening to the recordings of my conversation under the influence of the drug, I cannot discover that I was then any stupider than I am at ordinary times.)

(2) Visual impressions are greatly intensified and the eye recovers some of the perceptual innocence of childhood, when the sensum was not immediately and automatically subordinated to the concept. Interest in space is diminished and interest in time falls almost to zero.

(3) Though the intellect remains unimpaired and though perception is enormously improved, the will suffers a profound change for the worse. The mescalin taker sees no reason for doing anything in particular and finds most of the causes for which, at ordinary times, he was prepared to act and suffer, profoundly uninteresting. He can't be bothered with them, for the good reason that he has better things to think about.

(4) These better things may be experienced (as I experienced them) "out there," or "in here," or in both worlds, the inner and the outer, simultaneously or suc-

cessively. That they *are* better seems to be self-evident to all mescalin takers who come to the drug with a sound liver and an untroubled mind.

These effects of mescalin are the sort of effects you could expect to follow the administration of a drug having the power to impair the efficiency of the cerebral reducing valve. When the brain runs out of sugar, the undernourished ego grows weak, can't be bothered to undertake the necessary chores, and loses all interest in those spatial and temporal relationships which mean so much to an organism bent on getting on in the world. As Mind at Large seeps past the no longer watertight valve, all kinds of biologically useless things start to happen. In some cases there may be extra-sensory perceptions. Other persons discover a world of visionary beauty. To others again is revealed the glory, the infinite value and meaningfulness of naked existence, of the given, unconceptualized event. In the final stage of egolessness there is an "obscure knowledge" that All is in all—that All is actually each. This is as near, I take it, as a finite mind can ever come to "perceiving everything that is happening everywhere in the universe."

In this context, how significant is the enormous heightening, under mescalin, of the perception of color! For certain animals it is biologically very important to be able to distinguish certain hues. But beyond the limits of their utilitarian spectrum, most creatures are completely color blind. Bees, for example, spend most of their time "deflowering the fresh virgins of the spring"; but, as Von Frisch has shown, they can recognize only a very few colors. Man's highly developed color sense is a biological luxury—inestimably precious to him as an intellectual and spiritual being, but unnecessary to his survival as an animal. To judge by the adjectives which Homer puts into their mouths, the heroes of the Trojan War hardly excelled the bees in their capacity to distinguish colors. In this respect, at least, mankind's advance has been prodigious.

Mescalin raises all colors to a higher power and makes the percipient aware of innumerable fine shades of difference, to which, at ordinary times, he is completely blind. It would seem that, for Mind at Large, the so-called secondary characters of things are primary. Unlike Locke, it evidently feels that colors are more important, better worth attending to, than masses, positions and dimensions. Like mescalin takers, many mystics perceive supernaturally brilliant colors, not only with the inward eye, but even in the objective world around them. Similar reports are made by psychics and sensitives. There are certain mediums to whom the mescalin taker's brief revelation is a matter, during long periods, of daily and hourly experience.

From this long but indispensable excursion into the realm of theory, we may now return to the miraculous facts—four bamboo chair legs in the middle of a room. Like Wordsworth's daffodils, they brought all manner of wealth—the gift, beyond price, of a new direct insight into the very Nature of Things, together with a more modest treasure of understanding in the field, especially, of the arts.

A rose is a rose is a rose. But these chair legs were chair legs were St. Michael and all angels. Four or five hours after the event, when the effects of a cerebral sugar shortage were wearing off, I was taken for a little tour of the city, which included a visit, towards sundown, to what is modestly claimed to be the World's Biggest Drug Store. At the back of the W.B.D.S., among the toys, the greeting cards and the comics, stood a row, surprisingly enough, of art books. I picked up the first volume that came to hand. It was on Van Gogh, and the picture at which the book opened was "The Chair"—that astounding portrait of a *Ding an Sich*, which the mad painter saw, with a kind of adoring terror, and tried to render on his canvas. But it was a task to which the power even of genius proved wholly inadequate. The chair Van Gogh had seen was obviously the same in essence as the chair I had seen. But, though incomparably more real than the chairs of ordinary perception, the chair in his picture remained no more than an unusually expressive symbol of the fact. The fact had been manifested Suchness; this was only an emblem. Such emblems are sources of true knowledge about the Nature of Things, and this true knowledge may serve to prepare the mind which accepts it for immediate insights on its own account. But that is all. However expressive, symbols can never be the things they stand for.

It would be interesting, in this context, to make a study of the works of art available to the great knowers of Suchness. What sort of pictures did Eckhart look at? What sculptures and paintings played a part in the religious experience of St. John of the Cross, of Hakuin, of Hui-neng, of William Law? The questions are beyond my power to answer; but I strongly suspect that most of the great knowers of Suchness paid very little attention to art—some refusing to have anything to do with it at all, others being content with what a critical eye would regard as second-rate, or even, tenth-rate, works. (To a person whose transfigured and transfiguring mind can see the All in every *this*, the first-rateness or tenth-rateness of even a religious painting will be a matter of the most sovereign indifference.) Art, I suppose, is only for beginners, or else for those resolute dead-enders, who have made up their minds to be content with the *ersatz* of Suchness, with symbols rather than with what they signify, with the elegantly composed recipe in lieu of actual dinner.

I returned the Van Gogh to its rack and picked up the volume standing next to it. It was a book on Botticelli. I turned the pages. "The Birth of Venus"—never one of my favorites. "Mars and Venus," that loveliness so passionately denounced by poor Ruskin at the height of his long-drawn sexual tragedy. The marvelously rich and intricate "Calumny of Apelles." And then a somewhat less familiar and not very good picture, "Judith." My attention was arrested and I gazed in fascination, not at the pale neurotic heroine or her attendant, not at the victim's hairy head or the vernal landscape in the background, but at the purplish silk of Judith's pleated bodice and long wind-blown skirts.

This was something I had seen before—seen that very morning, between the flowers and the furniture, when I looked down by chance, and went on passionately staring by choice, at my own crossed legs. Those folds in the trousers—what a labyrinth of endlessly significant complexity! And the texture of the gray flannel—how rich, how deeply, mysteriously sumptuous! And here they were again, in Botticelli's picture.

Civilized human beings wear clothes, therefore there can be no portraiture, no mythological or historical storytelling without representations of folded textiles. But though it may account for the origins, mere tailoring can never explain the luxuriant development of drapery as a major theme of all the plastic arts. Artists, it is obvious, have always loved drapery for its own sake—or, rather, for their own. When you paint or carve drapery, you are painting or carving forms which, for all practical purposes, are non-representational—the kind of unconditioned forms on which artists even in the most naturalistic tradition like to let themselves go. In the average Madonna or Apostle the strictly human, fully representational element accounts for about ten per cent of the whole. All the rest consists of many colored variations on the inexhaustible theme of crumpled wool or linen. And these non-representational nine-tenths of a Madonna or an Apostle may be just as important qualitatively as they are in quantity. Very often they set the tone of the whole work of art, they state the key in which the theme is being rendered, they express the mood, the temperament, the attitude to life of the artist. Stoical serenity reveals itself in the smooth surfaces, the broad untortured folds of Piero's draperies. Torn between fact and wish, between cynicism and idealism, Bernini tempers the all but caricatural verisimilitude of his faces with enormous sartorial abstractions, which are the embodiment, in stone or bronze, of the everlasting commonplaces of rhetoric—the heroism, the holiness, the sublimity to which mankind perpetually aspires, for the most part in vain. And here are El Greco's disquietingly visceral skirts and mantles; here are the sharp, twisting, flame-like folds in which Cosimo Tura clothes his figures: in the first, traditional spirituality breaks down into a nameless physiological yearning; in the second, there writhes an agonized sense of the world's essential strangeness and hostility. Or consider Watteau; his men and women play lutes, get ready for balls and harlequinades, embark, on velvet lawns and under noble trees, for the Cythera of every lover's dream; their enormous melancholy and the flayed, excruciating sensibility of their creator find expression, not in the actions recorded, not in the gestures and the faces portrayed, but in the relief and texture of their taffeta skirts, their satin capes and doublets. Not an inch of smooth surface here, not a moment of peace or confidence, only a silken wilderness of countless tiny pleats and wrinkles, with an incessant modulation—inner uncertainty rendered with the perfect assurance of a master hand—of tone into tone, of one indeterminate color into another. In life, man proposes, God disposes. In the plastic arts the proposing is done by the subject matter; that which disposes is ultimately the artist's temperament, proximately (at least in portraiture, history and genre) the carved or painted drapery. Between them, these two may decree that a *fête galante* shall move to tears, that a crucifixion shall be serene to the point of cheerfulness, that a stigmatization shall be almost intolerably sexy, that the likeness of a prodigy of female brainlessness (I am thinking now of Ingres' incomparable Mme. Moitessier) shall express the austerest, the most uncompromising intellectuality.

But this is not the whole story. Draperies, as I had now discovered, are much more than devices for the introduction of non-representational forms into naturalistic paintings and sculptures. What the rest of us see only under the influence of mescalin, the artist is congenitally equipped to see all the time. His perception is not limited to what is biologically or socially useful. A little of the knowledge belonging to Mind at Large oozes past the reducing valve of brain and ego, into his consciousness. It is a knowledge of the intrinsic significance of every existent. For the artist as for the mescalin taker draperies are living hieroglyphs that stand in some peculiarly expressive way for the unfathomable mystery of pure being. More even than the chair, though less perhaps than those wholly supernatural flowers, the folds of my gray flannel trousers were charged with "is-ness." To what they owed this privileged status, I cannot say. Is it, perhaps, because the forms of folded drapery are so strange and dramatic that they catch the eye and in this way force the miraculous fact of sheer existence upon the attention? Who knows? What is important is less the reason for the experience than the experience itself. Poring over Judith's skirts, there in the World's Biggest Drug Store, I knew that Botticelli—and not Botticelli alone, but many others too—had looked at draperies with the same transfigured and transfiguring eyes as had been mine that morning. They had seen the *Istigkeit*, the Allness and Infinity of folded cloth and had done their best to render it in paint or stone. Necessarily, of course, without success. For the glory and the wonder of pure existence belong to another order, beyond the power of even the highest art to express. But in Judith's skirt I could clearly see what, if I had been a painter of genius, I might have made of my old gray flannels. Not much, heaven knows, in comparison with the reality; but enough to delight generation after generation of beholders, enough to make them understand at least a little of the true significance of what, in our pathetic imbecility, we call "mere things" and disregard in favor of television.

"This is how one ought to see," I kept saying as I looked down at my trousers, or glanced at the jeweled books in the shelves, at the legs of my infinitely more than Van-Goghian chair. "This is how one ought to see, how things really are." And yet there were reservations. For if one always saw like this, one would never want to do anything else. Just looking, just being the divine Not-self of flower, of book, of chair, of flannel. That would be enough. But in that case what about other people? What about human relations? In the recording of that morning's conversations I find the question constantly repeated, "What about human relations?" How could one reconcile this timeless bliss of seeing as one ought to see with the temporal duties of doing what one ought to do and feeling as one ought to feel? "One ought to be able," I said, "to see these trousers as infinitely important and human beings as still more infinitely important." One ought—but in practice it seemed to be impossible. This participation in the manifest glory of things left no room, so to speak, for the ordinary, the necessary concerns of human existence, above all for concerns involving persons. For persons are selves and, in one respect at least, I was now a Not-self, simultaneously perceiving and being the Not-self of the things around me. To this new-born Not-self, the behavior, the appearance, the very thought of the self it had momentarily ceased to be, and of other selves, its one-time fellows, seemed not indeed distasteful (for distastefulness was not one of the categories in terms of which I was thinking), but enormously irrelevant. Compelled by the investigator to analyze and report on what I was doing (and how I longed to be left alone with Eternity in a flower, Infinity in four chair legs and the Absolute in the folds of a pair of flannel trousers!), I realized that I was deliberately avoiding the eyes of those who were with me in the room, deliberately refraining from being too much aware of them. One was my wife, the other a man I respected and greatly liked; but both belonged to the world from which, for the moment, mescalin had delivered me —the world of selves, of time, of moral judgments and utilitarian considerations, the world (and it was this aspect of human life which I wished, above all else, to forget) of self-assertion, of cocksureness, of overvalued words and idolatrously worshiped notions.

At this stage of the proceedings I was handed a large colored reproduction of the well-known self-portrait by Cézanne—the head and shoulders of a man in a large straw hat, red-cheeked, red-lipped, with rich black whiskers and a dark unfriendly eye. It is a magnificent painting; but it was not as a painting that I now saw it. For the head promptly took on a third dimension and came to life as a small goblin-like man looking out through a window in the page before me. I started to laugh. And when they asked me why, "What pretensions!" I kept repeating. "Who on earth does he think he is?" The question was not addressed to Cézanne in particular, but to the human species at large. Who did they all think they were?

"It's like Arnold Bennett in the Dolomites," I said, suddenly remembering a scene, happily immortalized in a snapshot, of A.B., some four or five years before his death, toddling along a wintry road at Cortina d'Ampezzo. Around him lay the virgin snow; in the background was a more than gothic aspiration of red crags. And there was dear, kind, unhappy A.B., consciously overacting the role of his favorite character in fiction, himself, the Card in person. There he went, toddling slowly in the bright Alpine sunshine, his thumbs in the armholes of a yellow waistcoat which bulged, a little lower down, with the graceful curve of a Regency bow window at Brighton—his head thrown back as though to aim some stammered utterance, howitzer-like, at the blue dome of heaven. What he actually said, I have forgotten; but what his whole manner, air and posture fairly shouted was, "I'm as good as those damned mountains." And in some ways, of course, he was infinitely better; but not, as he knew very well, in the way his favorite character in fiction liked to imagine.

Successfully (whatever that may mean) or unsuccessfully, we all overact the part of our favorite character in fiction. And the fact, the almost infinitely unlikely fact, of actually being Cézanne makes no difference. For the consummate painter, with his little pipeline to Mind at Large by-passing the brain valve and ego-filter, was also and just as genuinely this whiskered goblin with the unfriendly eye.

For relief I turned back to the folds in my trousers. "This is how one ought to see," I repeated yet again. And I might have added, "These are the sort of things one ought to look at." Things without pretensions, satisfied to be merely themselves, sufficient in their Suchness, not acting a part, not trying, insanely, to go it alone, in isolation from the Dharma-Body, in Luciferian defiance of the grace of God.

"The nearest approach to this," I said, "would be a Vermeer."

Yes, a Vermeer. For that mysterious artist was trebly gifted—with the vision that perceives the Dharma-Body as the hedge at the bottom of the garden, with the talent to render as much of that vision as the limitations of human capacity permit, and with the prudence to confine himself in his paintings to the more manageable aspects of reality; for though Vermeer represented human beings, he was always a painter of still life. Cézanne, who told his female sitters to do their best to look like apples, tried to paint portraits in the same spirit. But his pippin-like women are more nearly related to Plato's Ideas than to the Dharma-Body in the hedge. They are Eternity and Infinity seen, not in sand or flower, but in the abstractions of some very superior brand of geometry. Vermeer never asked his girls to look like apples. On the contrary, he insisted on their being girls to the very limit—but always with the proviso that they refrain from behaving girlishly. They might sit or quietly stand but never giggle, never display self-consciousness, never say their prayers or pine for absent sweethearts, never gossip, never gaze enviously at other women's babies, never flirt, never love or hate or work. In the act of doing any of these things they would doubtless become more intensely themselves, but would cease, for that very reason, to manifest their divine essential Not-self. In Blake's phrase, the doors of Vermeer's perception were only partially cleansed. A single panel had become almost perfectly transparent; the rest of the door was still muddy. The essential Not-self could be perceived very clearly in things and in living creatures on the hither side of good and evil. In human beings it was visible only when they were in repose, their minds untroubled, their bodies motionless. In these circumstances Vermeer could see Suchness in all its heavenly beauty—could see and, in some small measure, render it in a subtle and sumptuous still life. Vermeer is undoubtedly the greatest painter of human still lives. But there have been others, for example, Vermeer's French contemporaries, the Le Nain brothers. They set out, I suppose, to be genre painters; but what they actually produced was a series of human still lives, in which their cleansed perception of the infinite significance of all things is rendered not, as with Vermeer, by subtle enrichment of color and texture, but by a heightened clarity, an obsessive distinctness of form, within an austere, almost monochromatic tonality. In our own day we have had Vuillard, the painter, at his best, of unforgettably splendid pictures of the Dharma-Body manifested in a bourgeois bedroom, of the Absolute blazing away in the midst of some stockbroker's family in a suburban garden, taking tea.

> Ce qui fait que l'ancien bandagiste renie
> Le comptoir dont le faste alléchait les passants,
> C'est son jardin d'Auteuil, où, veufs de tout encens,
> Les Zinnias ont l'air d'être en tôle vernie.

For Laurent Tailhade the spectacle was merely obscene. But if the retired rubber goods merchant had sat still enough, Vuillard would have seen in him only the Dharma-Body, would have painted, in the zinnias, the goldfish pool, the villa's Moorish tower and Chinese lanterns, a corner of Eden before the Fall.

But meanwhile my question remained unanswered. How was this cleansed perception to be reconciled with a proper concern with human relations, with the necessary chores and duties, to say nothing of charity and practical compassion? The age-old debate between the actives and the contemplatives was being renewed—renewed, so far as I was concerned, with an unprecedented poignancy. For until this morning I had known contemplation only in its humbler, its more ordinary forms—as discursive thinking; as a rapt absorption in poetry or painting or music; as a patient waiting upon those inspirations, without which even the prosiest writer cannot hope to accomplish anything; as occasional glimpses, in Nature, of Wordsworth's "something far more deeply interfused"; as systematic silence leading, sometimes, to hints of an "obscure knowledge." But now I knew contemplation at its height. At its height, but not yet in its fullness. For in its fullness the way of Mary includes the way of Martha and raises it, so to speak, to its own higher power. Mescalin opens up the way of Mary, but shuts the door on that of Martha. It gives access to contemplation—but to a contemplation that is incompatible with action and even with the will to action, the very thought of action. In the intervals between his revelations the mescalin taker is apt to feel that, though in one way everything is supremely as it should be, in another there is something wrong. His problem is essentially the same as that which confronts the quietist, the *arhat* and, on another level, the landscape painter and the painter of human still lives. Mescalin can never solve that problem; it can only pose it, apocalyptically, for those to whom it had never before presented itself. The full and final solution can be found only by those who are prepared to implement the right kind of *Weltanschauung* by means of the right kind of behavior and the right kind of constant and unstrained alertness. Over against the quietist stands the active-contemplative, the saint, the man who, in Eckhart's phrase, is ready to come down from the seventh heaven in order to bring a cup of water to his sick brother. Over against the *arhat*, retreating from appearances into an entirely transcendental Nirvana, stands the Bodhisattva, for whom Suchness and the world of contingencies are one, and for whose boundless compassion every one of those contingencies is an occasion not only for transfiguring insight, but also for the most practical charity. And in the universe of art, over against Vermeer and the other painters of human still lives, over against the masters of Chinese and Japanese landscape painting, over against Constable and Turner, against Sisley and Seurat and Cézanne, stands the all-inclusive art of Rembrandt. These are enormous names, inaccessible eminences. For myself, on this memorable May morning, I could only be grateful for an experience which had shown me, more clearly than I had ever seen it before, the true nature of the challenge and the completely liberating response.

Let me add, before we leave this subject, that there is no form of contemplation, even the most quietistic, which is without its ethical values. Half at least of all morality is negative and consists in keeping out of mischief. The Lord's Prayer is less than fifty words long, and six of those words are devoted to asking God not to lead us into temptation. The one-sided contemplative leaves undone many things that he ought to do; but to make up for it, he refrains from doing a host of things he ought not to do. The sum of evil, Pascal remarked, would be much diminished if men could only learn to sit quietly in their rooms. The contemplative whose perception has been cleansed does not have to stay in his room. He can go about his business, so completely satisfied to see and be a part of the divine Order of Things that he will never even be tempted to indulge in what Traherne called "the dirty Devices of the world." When we feel ourselves to be sole heirs of the universe, when "the sea flows in our veins . . . and the stars are our jewels," when all things are perceived as infinite and holy, what motive can we have for covetousness or self-assertion, for the pursuit of power or the drearier forms of pleasure? Contemplatives are not likely to become gamblers, or procurers, or drunkards; they do not as a rule preach intolerance, or make war; do not find it necessary to rob, swindle or grind the faces of the poor. And to these enormous negative virtues we may add another which, though hard to define, is both positive and

43

important. The *arhat* and the quietist may not practice contemplation in its fullness; but if they practice it at all, they may bring back enlightening reports of another, a transcendent country of the mind; and if they practice it in the height, they will become conduits through which some beneficent influence can flow out of that other country into a world of darkened selves, chronically dying for lack of it.

Meanwhile I had turned, at the investigator's request, from the portrait of Cézanne to what was going on, inside my head, when I shut my eyes. This time, the inscape was curiously unrewarding. The field of vision was filled with brightly colored, constantly changing structures that seemed to be made of plastic or enameled tin.

"Cheap," I commented. "Trivial. Like things in a five-and-ten." And all this shoddiness existed in a closed, cramped universe. "It's as though one were below decks in a ship," I said. "A five-and-ten-cent ship."

And as I looked, it became very clear that this five-and-ten-cent ship was in some way connected with human pretensions, with the portrait of Cézanne, with A.B. among the Dolomites overacting his favorite character in fiction. This suffocating interior of a dime-store ship was my own personal self; these gimcrack mobiles of tin and plastic were my personal contributions to the universe.

I felt the lesson to be salutary, but was sorry, none the less, that it had had to be administered at this moment and in this form. As a rule the mescalin taker discovers an inner world as manifestly a datum, as self-evidently "infinite and holy," as that transfigured outer world which I had seen with my eyes open. From the first, my own case had been different. Mescalin had endowed me temporarily with the power to see things with my eyes shut; but it could not, or at least on this occasion did not, reveal an inscape remotely comparable to my flowers or chair or flannels "out there." What it had allowed me to perceive inside was not the Dharma-Body, in images, but my own mind; not Suchness, but a set of symbols—in other words, a homemade substitute for Suchness.

Most visualizers are transformed by mescalin into visionaries. Some of them—and they are perhaps more numerous than is generally supposed—require no transformation; they are visionaries all the time. The mental species to which Blake belonged is fairly widely distributed even in the urban-industrial societies of the present day. The poet-artist's uniqueness does not consist in the fact that (to quote from his *Descriptive Catalogue*) he actually *saw* "those wonderful originals called in the Sacred Scriptures the Cherubim." It does not consist in the fact that "these wonderful originals seen in my visions, were some of them one hundred feet in height . . . all containing mythological and recondite meaning." It consists solely in his ability to render, in words or (somewhat less successfully) in line and color, some hint at least of a not excessively uncommon experience. The untalented visionary may perceive an inner reality no less tremendous, beautiful and significant than the world beheld by Blake; but he lacks altogether the ability to express, in literary or plastic symbols, what he has seen.

From the records of religion and the surviving monuments of poetry and the plastic arts it is very plain that, at most times and in most places, men have attached more importance to the inscape than to objective existents, have felt that what they saw with their eyes shut possessed a spiritually higher significance than what they saw with their eyes open. The reason? Familiarity breeds contempt, and how to survive is a problem ranging in urgency from the chronically tedious to the excruciating. The outer world is what we wake up to every morning of our lives, is the place where, willy-nilly, we must try to make our living. In the inner world there is neither work nor monotony. We visit it only in dreams and musings, and its strangeness is such that we never find the same world on two successive occasions. What wonder, then, if human beings in their search for the divine have generally preferred to look within! Generally, but not always. In their art no less than in their religion, the Taoists and the Zen Buddhists looked beyond visions to the Void, and through the Void at "the ten thousand things" of objective reality. Because of their doctrine of the Word made flesh, Christians should have been able, from the first, to adopt a similar attitude towards the universe around them. But because of the doctrine of the Fall, they found it very hard to do so. As recently as three hundred years ago an expression of thoroughgoing world denial and even world condemnation was both orthodox and comprehensible. "We should feel wonder at nothing at all in Nature except only the Incarnation of Christ." In the seventeenth century, Lallemant's phrase seemed to make sense. Today it has the ring of madness.

In China the rise of landscape painting to the rank of a major art form took place about a thousand, in Japan about six hundred and in Europe about three hundred, years ago. The equation of Dharma-Body with hedge was made by those Zen Masters, who wedded Taoist naturalism with Buddhist transcendentalism. It was, therefore, only in the Far East that landscape painters consciously regarded their art as religious. In the West religious painting was a matter of portraying sacred personages, of illustrating hallowed texts. Landscape painters regarded themselves as secularists. Today we recognize in Seurat one of the supreme masters of what may be called mystical landscape painting. And yet this man who was able, more effectively than any other, to render the One in the many, became quite indignant when somebody praised him for the "poetry" of his work. "I merely apply the System," he protested. In other words he was merely a *pointilliste* and, in his own eyes, nothing else. A similar anecdote is told of John Constable. One day towards the end of his life, Blake met Constable at Hampstead and was shown one of the younger artist's sketches. In spite of his contempt for naturalistic art, the old visionary knew a good thing when he saw it—except, of course, when it was by Rubens. "This is not drawing," he cried, "this is inspiration!" "I had meant it to be drawing," was Constable's characteristic answer. Both men were right. It *was* drawing, precise and veracious, and at the same time it *was* inspiration —inspiration of an order at least as high as Blake's. The pine trees on the Heath had actually been seen as identical with the Dharma-Body. The sketch was a rendering, necessarily imperfect but still profoundly impressive, of what a cleansed perception had revealed to the open eyes of a great painter. From a contemplation, in the tradition of Wordsworth and Whitman, of the Dharma-Body as hedge, and from visions, such as Blake's, of the "wonderful originals" within the mind, contemporary poets have retreated into an investigation of the personal, as opposed to the more than personal, subconscious and to a rendering, in highly abstract terms, not of the given, objective fact, but of mere scientific and theological notions. And something similar has happened in the field of painting, where we have witnessed a general retreat from landscape, the predominant art form of the nineteenth century. This retreat from landscape has not been into that other, inner divine Datum, with which most of the traditional schools of the past were concerned, that Archetypal World, where men have always found the raw materials of myth and religion. No, it has been a retreat from the outward Datum into the personal subconscious, into a mental world more squalid and more tightly closed than even the world of conscious personality. These contraptions of tin and highly colored plastic —where had I seen them before? In every picture gallery that exhibits the latest in nonrepresentational art.

And now someone produced a phonograph and put a record on the turntable. I listened with pleasure, but experienced nothing comparable to my seen apocalypses of flowers or flannel. Would a naturally gifted musician *hear* the revelations which, for me, had been exclusively visual? It would be interesting to make the experiment. Meanwhile, though not transfigured, though retaining its normal quality and intensity, the music contributed not a little to my understanding of what had happened to me and of the wider problems which those happenings had raised.

Instrumental music, oddly enough, left me rather cold. Mozart's C-Minor Piano Concerto was interrupted after the first movement, and a recording of some madrigals by Gesualdo took its place.

"These voices," I said appreciatively, "these voices—they're a kind of bridge back to the human world."

And a bridge they remained even while singing the most startlingly chromatic of the mad prince's compositions. Through the uneven phrases of the madrigals, the music pursued its course, never sticking to the same key for two bars together. In Gesualdo, that fantastic character out of a Webster melodrama, psychological disintegration had exaggerated, had pushed to the extreme limit, a tendency inherent in modal as opposed to fully tonal music. The resulting works sounded as though they might have been written by the later Schoenberg.

"And yet," I felt myself constrained to say, as I listened to these strange products of a Counter-Reformation psychosis working upon a late medieval art form, "and yet it does not matter that he's all in bits. The whole is disorganized. But each individual fragment is in order, is a representative of a Higher Order. The Highest Order prevails even in the disintegration. The totality is present even in the broken pieces. More clearly present, perhaps, than in a completely coherent work. At least you aren't lulled into a sense of false security by some merely human, merely fabricated order. You have to rely on your immediate perception of the ultimate order. So in a certain sense disintegration may have its advantages. But of course it's dangerous, horribly dangerous. Suppose you couldn't get back, out of the chaos . . ."

From Gesualdo's madrigals we jumped, across a gulf of three centuries, to Alban Berg and the *Lyric Suite*.

"This," I announced in advance, "is going to be hell."

But, as it turned out, I was wrong. Actually the music sounded rather funny. Dredged up from the personal subconscious, agony succeeded twelve-tone agony; but what struck me was only the essential incongruity between a psychological disintegration even completer than Gesualdo's and the prodigious resources, in talent and technique, employed in its expression.

"Isn't he sorry for himself!" I commented with a derisive lack of sympathy. And then, *"Katzenmusik—* learned *Katzenmusik."* And finally, after a few more minutes of the anguish, "Who cares what his feelings are? Why can't he pay attention to something else?"

As a criticism of what is undoubtedly a very remarkable work, it was unfair and inadequate—but not, I think, irrelevant. I cite it for what it is worth and because that is how, in a state of pure contemplation, I reacted to the *Lyric Suite*.

When it was over, the investigator suggested a walk in the garden. I was willing; and though my body seemed to have dissociated itself almost completely from my mind—or, to be more accurate, though my awareness of the transfigured outer world was no longer accompanied by an awareness of my physical organism—I found myself able to get up, open the French window and walk out with only a minimum of hesitation. It was odd, of course, to feel that "I" was not the same as these arms and legs "out there," as this wholly objective trunk and neck and even head. It was odd; but one soon got used to it. And anyhow the body seemed perfectly well able to look after itself. In reality, of course, it always does look after itself. All that the conscious ego can do is to formulate wishes, which are then carried out by forces which it controls very little and understands not at all. When it does anything more—when it tries too hard, for example, when it worries, when it becomes apprehensive about the future—it lowers the effectiveness of those forces and may even cause the devitalized body to fall ill. In my present state, awareness was not referred to as ego; it was, so to speak, on its own. This meant that the physiological intelligence controlling the body was also on its own. For the moment that interfering neurotic who, in waking hours, tries to run the show, was blessedly out of the way.

From the French window I walked out under a kind of pergola covered in part by a climbing rose tree, in part by laths, one inch wide with half an inch of space between them. The sun was shining and the shadows of the laths made a zebra-like pattern on the ground and across the seat and back of a garden chair, which was standing at this end of the pergola. That chair—shall I ever forget it? Where the shadows fell on the canvas upholstery, stripes of a deep but glowing indigo alternated with stripes of an incandescence so intensely bright that it was hard to believe that they could be made of anything but blue fire. For what seemed an immensely long time I gazed without knowing, even without wishing to know, what it was that confronted me. At any other time I would have seen a chair barred with alternate light and shade. Today the percept had swallowed up the concept. I was so completely absorbed in looking, so thunderstruck by what I actually saw, that I could not be aware of anything else. Garden furniture, laths, sunlight, shadow—these were no more than names and notions, mere verbalizations, for utilitarian or scientific purposes, after the event. The event was this succession of azure furnace doors separated by gulfs of unfathomable gentian. It was inexpressibly wonderful, wonderful to the point, almost, of being terrifying. And suddenly I had an inkling of what it must feel like to be mad. Schizophrenia has its heavens as well as its hells and purgatories. I remember what an old friend, dead these many years, told me about his mad wife. One day in the early stages of the disease, when she still had her lucid intervals he had gone to talk to her about their children. She listened for a time, then cut him short. How could he bear to waste his time on a couple of absent children, when all that really mattered, here and now, was the unspeakable beauty of the patterns he made, in this brown tweed jacket, every time he moved his arms? Alas, this paradise of cleansed perception, of pure one-sided contemplation, was not to endure. The blissful intermissions became rarer, became briefer, until finally there were no more of them; there was only horror.

Most takers of mescalin experience only the heavenly part of schizophrenia. The drug brings hell and purgatory only to those who have had a recent case of jaundice, or who suffer from periodical depressions or a chronic anxiety. If, like the other drugs of remotely comparable power, mescalin were notoriously toxic, the taking of it would be enough, of itself, to cause anxiety. But the reasonably healthy person knows in advance that, so far as he is concerned, mescalin is completely innocuous, that its effects will pass off after eight or ten hours, leaving no hangover and consequently no craving for a renewal of the dose. Fortified by this knowledge, he embarks upon the experiment without fear—in other words, without any disposition to convert an unprecedentedly strange and other than human experience into something appalling, something actually diabolical.

Confronted by a chair which looked like the Last Judgment—or, to be more accurate, by a Last Judgment which, after a long time and with considerable difficulty, I recognized as a chair—I found myself all at once on the brink of panic. This, I suddenly felt, was going too far. Too far, even though the going was into intenser beauty, deeper significance. The fear, as I analyze it in retrospect, was of being overwhelmed, of disintegrating under a pressure of reality greater than a mind, accustomed to living most of the time in a cosy world of symbols, could possibly bear. The literature of religious experience abounds in references to the pains and terrors overwhelming those who have come, too suddenly, face to face with some manifestation of the *Mysterium tremendum*. In theological language, this fear is due to the incompatibility between man's egotism and the divine purity, between man's self-aggravated separateness and the infinity of God. Following Boehme and William Law, we may say that, by unregenerate souls, the divine Light at its full blaze can be apprehended only as a burning, purgatorial fire. An almost identical doctrine is to be found in *The Tibetan Book of the Dead*, where the departed soul is described as shrinking in agony from the Pure Light of the Void, and even from the lesser, tempered Lights, in order to rush headlong into the comforting darkness of selfhood as a reborn human being, or even as a beast, an unhappy ghost, a denizen of hell. Anything rather than the burning brightness of unmitigated Reality—anything!

The schizophrenic is a soul not merely unregenerate, but desperately sick into the bargain. His sickness consists in the inability to take refuge from inner and outer reality (as the sane person habitually does) in the homemade universe of common sense—the strictly human world of useful notions, shared symbols and socially acceptable conventions. The schizophrenic is like a man permanently under the influence of mescalin, and therefore unable to shut off the experience of a reality which he is not holy enough to live with, which he cannot explain away because it is the most stubborn of primary facts, and which, because it never permits him to look at the world with merely human eyes, scares him into interpreting its unremitting strangeness, its burning intensity of significance, as the manifestations of human or even cosmic malevolence, calling for the most desperate countermeasures, from murderous violence at one end of the scale to catatonia, or psychological suicide, at the other. And once embarked upon the downward, the infernal road, one would never be able to stop. That, now, was only too obvious.

"If you started in the wrong way," I said in answer to the investigator's questions, "everything that happened would be a proof of the conspiracy against you. It would all be self-validating. You couldn't draw a breath without knowing it was part of the plot."

"So you think you know where madness lies?"

My answer was a convinced and heartfelt, "Yes."

"And you couldn't control it?"

"No I couldn't control it. If one began with fear and hate as the major premise, one would have to go on to the conclusion."

"Would you be able," my wife asked, "to fix your attention on what *The Tibetan Book of the Dead* calls the Clear Light?"

I was doubtful.

"Would it keep the evil away, if you could hold it? Or would you not be able to hold it?"

I considered the question for some time. "Perhaps," I answered at last, "perhaps I could—but only if there were somebody there to tell me about the Clear Light. One couldn't do it by oneself. That's the point, I suppose, of the Tibetan ritual—someone sitting there all the time and telling you what's what."

After listening to the record of this part of the experiment, I took down my copy of Evans-Wentz's edition of *The Tibetan Book of the Dead,* and opened at random. "O nobly born, let not thy mind be distracted." That was the problem—to remain undistracted. Undistracted by the memory of past sins, by imagined pleasure, by the bitter aftertaste of old wrongs and humiliations, by all the fears and hates and cravings that ordinarily eclipse the Light. What those Buddhist monks did for the dying and the dead, might not the modern psychiatrist do for the insane? Let there be a voice to assure them, by day and even while they are asleep, that in spite of all the terror, all the bewilderment and confusion, the ultimate Reality remains unshakably itself and is of the same substance as the inner light of even the most cruelly tormented mind. By means of such devices as recorders, clock-controlled switches, public address systems and pillow speakers it should be very easy to keep the inmates of even an understaffed institution constantly reminded of this primordial fact. Perhaps a few of the lost souls might in this way be helped to win some measure of control over the universe—at once beautiful and appalling, but always other than human, always totally incomprehensible—in which they find themselves condemned to live.

None too soon, I was steered away from the disquieting splendors of my garden chair. Drooping in green parabolas from the hedge, the ivy fronds shone with a kind of glassy, jade-like radiance. A moment later a clump of Red Hot Pokers, in full bloom, had exploded into my field of vision. So passionately alive that they seemed to be standing on the very brink of utterance, the flowers strained upwards into the blue. Like the chair under the laths, they protected too much. I looked down at the leaves and discovered a cavernous intricacy of the most delicate green lights and shadows, pulsing with undecipherable mystery.

> Roses:
> The flowers are easy to paint,
> The leaves difficult.

Shiki's *haiku* (which I quote in R. H. Blyth's translation) expresses, by indirection, exactly what I then felt—the excessive, the too obvious glory of the flowers, as contrasted with the subtler miracle of their foliage.

We walked out into the street. A large pale blue automobile was standing at the curb. At the sight of it, I was suddenly overcome by enormous merriment. What complacency, what an absurd self-satisfaction beamed from those bulging surfaces of glossiest enamel! Man had created the thing in his own image—or rather in the image of his favorite character in fiction. I laughed till the tears ran down my cheeks.

We re-entered the house. A meal had been prepared. Somebody, who was not yet identical with myself, fell to with ravenous appetite. From a considerable distance and without much interest, I looked on.

When the meal had been eaten, we got into the car and went for a drive. The effects of the mescalin were already on the decline: but the flowers in the gardens still trembled on the brink of being supernatural, the pepper trees and carobs along the side streets still manifestly belonged to some sacred grove. Eden alternated with Dodona. Yggdrasil with the mystic Rose. And then, abruptly, we were at an intersection, waiting to cross Sunset Boulevard. Before us the cars were rolling by in a steady stream—thousands of them, all bright and shiny like an advertiser's dream and each more ludicrous than the last. Once again I was convulsed with laughter.

The Red Sea of traffic parted at last, and we crossed into another oasis of trees and lawns and roses. In a few minutes we had climbed to a vantage point in the hills, and there was the city spread out beneath us. Rather disappointingly, it looked very like the city I had seen on other occasions. So far as I was concerned, transfiguration was proportional to distance. The nearer, the more divinely other. This vast, dim panorama was hardly different from itself.

We drove on, and so long as we remained in the hills, with view succeeding distant view, significance was at its everyday level, well below transfiguration point. The magic began to work again only when we turned down into a new suburb and were gliding between two rows of houses. Here, in spite of the peculiar hideousness of the architecture, there were renewals of transcendental otherness, hints of the morning's heaven. Brick chimneys and green composition roofs glowed in the sunshine, like fragments of the New Jerusalem. And all at once I saw what Guardi had seen and (with what incomparable skill) had so often rendered in his paintings—a stucco wall with a shadow slanting across it, blank but unforgettably beautiful, empty but charged with all the meaning and the mystery of existence. The revelation dawned and was gone again within a fraction of a second. The car had moved on; time was uncovering another manifestation of the eternal Suchness. "Within sameness there is difference. But that difference should be different from sameness is in no wise the intention of all the Buddhas. Their intention is both totality and differentiation." This bank of red and white geraniums, for ex-ample—it was entirely different from that stucco wall a hundred yards up the road. But the "is-ness" of both was the same, the eternal quality of their transience was the same.

An hour later, with ten more miles and the visit to the World's Biggest Drug Store safely behind us, we were back at home, and I had returned to that reassuring but profoundly unsatisfactory state known as "being in one's right mind."

That humanity at large will ever be able to dispense with Artificial Paradises seems very unlikely. Most men and women lead lives at the worst so painful, at the best so monotonous, poor and limited that the urge to escape, the longing to transcend themselves if only for a few moments, is and has always been one of the principal appetites of the soul. Art and religion, carnivals and saturnalia, dancing and listening to oratory—all these have served, in H. G. Wells's phrase, as Doors in the Wall. And for private, for everyday use there have always been chemical intoxicants. All the vegetable sedatives and narcotics, all the euphorics that grow on trees, the hallucinogens that ripen in berries or can be squeezed from roots—all, without exception, have been known and systematically used by human beings from time immemorial. And to these natural modifiers of consciousness modern science has added its quota of synthetics—chloral, for example, and benzedrine, the bromides and the barbiturates.

Most of these modifiers of consciousness cannot now be taken except under doctor's orders, or else illegally and at considerable risk. For unrestricted use the West has permitted only alcohol and tobacco. All the other chemical Doors in the Wall are labeled Dope, and their unauthorized takers are Fiends.

We now spend a good deal more on drink and smoke than we spend on education. This, of course, is not surprising. The urge to escape from selfhood and the environment is in almost everyone almost all the time. The urge to do something for the young is strong only in parents, and in them only for the few years during which their children go to school. Equally unsurprising is the current attitude towards drink and smoke. In spite of the growing army of hopeless alcoholics, in spite of the hundreds of thousands of persons annually maimed or killed by drunken drivers, popular comedians still crack jokes about alcohol and its addicts. And in spite of the evidence linking cigarettes with lung cancer, practically everybody regards tobacco smoking as being hardly less normal and natural than eating. From the point of view of the rationalist utilitarian this may seem odd. For the historian, it is exactly what you would expect. A firm conviction of the material reality of Hell never prevented medieval Christians from doing what their ambition, lust or covetousness suggested. Lung cancer, traffic accidents and the millions of miserable and misery-creating alcoholics are facts even more certain than was, in Dante's day, the fact of the Inferno. But all such facts are remote and unsubstantial compared with the near, felt fact of a craving, here and now, for release or sedation, for a drink or a smoke.

Ours is the age, among other things, of the automobile and of rocketing population. Alcohol is incompatible with safety on the roads, and its production, like that of tobacco, condemns to virtual sterility many millions of acres of the most fertile soil. The problems raised by alcohol and tobacco cannot, it goes without saying, be solved by prohibition. The universal and ever-present urge to self-transcendence is not to be abolished by slamming the currently popular Doors in the Wall. The only reasonable policy is to open other, better doors in the hope of inducing men and women to exchange their old bad habits for new and less harmful ones. Some of these other, better doors will be social and technological in nature, others religious or psychological, others dietetic, educational, athletic. But the need for frequent chemical vacations from intolerable selfhood and repulsive surroundings will undoubtedly remain. What is needed is a new drug which will relieve and console our suffering species without doing more harm in the long run than it does good in the short. Such a drug must be potent in minute doses and synthesizable. If it does not possess these qualities, its production, like that of wine, beer, spirits and tobacco will interfere with the raising of indispensable food and fibers. It must be less toxic than opium or cocaine, less likely to produce undesirable social consequences than alcohol or the barbiturates, less inimical to heart and lungs than the tars and nicotine of cigarettes. And, on the positive side, it should produce changes in consciousness more interesting, more intrinsically valuable than mere sedation or dreaminess, delusions of omnipotence or release from inhibition.

To most people, mescalin is almost completely innocuous. Unlike alcohol, it does not drive the taker into the kind of uninhibited action which results in brawls, crimes of violence and traffic accidents. A man under the influence of mescalin quietly minds his own business. Moreover, the business he minds is an experience of the most enlightening kind, which does not have to be paid for (and this is surely important) by a compensatory hangover. Of the long-range consequences of regular mescalin taking we know very little. The Indians who consume peyote buttons do not seem to be physically or morally degraded by the habit. However, the available evidence is still scarce and sketchy.*

Although obviously superior to cocaine, opium, alcohol and tobacco, mescalin is not yet the ideal drug. Along with the happily transfigured majority of mescalin takers there is a minority that finds in the drug only hell or purgatory. Moreover, for a drug that is to be used, like alcohol, for general consumption, its effects last for an inconveniently long time. But chemistry and physi-

* In his monograph, *Menomini Peyotism*, published (December, 1952) in the Transactions of the American Philosophical Society, Professor J. S. Slotkin has written that "the habitual use of Peyote does not seem to produce any increased tolerance or dependence. I know many people who have been Peyotists for forty to fifty years. The amount of Peyote they use depends upon the solemnity of the occasion; in general they do not take any more Peyote now than they did years ago. Also, there is sometimes an interval of a month or more between rites, and they go without Peyote during this period without feeling any craving for it. Personally, even after a series of rites occurring on four successive weekends, I neither increased the amount of Peyote consumed nor felt any continued need for it." It is evidently with good reason that "Peyote has never been legally declared a narcotic, or its use prohibited by the federal government." However, "during the long history of Indian-white contact, white officials have usually tried to suppress the use of Peyote, because it has been conceived to violate their own mores. But these attempts have always failed." In a footnote Dr. Slotkin adds that "it is amazing to hear the fantastic stories about the effects of Peyote and the nature of the ritual, which are told by the white and Catholic Indian officials in the Menomini Reservation. None of them have had the slightest first-hand experience with the plant or with the religion, yet some fancy themselves to be authorities and write official reports on the subject."

ology are capable nowadays of practically anything. If the psychologists and sociologists will define the ideal, the neurologists and pharmacologists can be relied upon to discover the means whereby that ideal can be realized or at least (for perhaps this kind of ideal can never, in the very nature of things, be fully realized) more nearly approached than in the wine-bibbing past, the whisky-drinking, marijuana-smoking and barbiturate-swallowing present.

The urge to transcend self-conscious selfhood is, as I have said, a principal appetite of the soul. When, for whatever reason, men and women fail to transcend themselves by means of worship, good works and spiritual exercises, they are apt to resort to religion's chemical surrogates—alcohol and "goof pills" in the modern West, alcohol and opium in the East, hashish in the Mohammedan world, alcohol and marijuana in Central America, alcohol and coca in the Andes, alcohol and the barbiturates in the more up-to-date regions of South America. In *Poisons Sacrés, Ivresses Divines* Philippe de Félice has written at length and with a wealth of documentation on the immemorial connection between religion and the taking of drugs. Here, in summary or in direct quotation, are his conclusions. The employment for religious purposes of toxic substances is "extraordinarily widespread. . . . The practices studied in this volume can be observed in every region of the earth, among primitives no less than among those who have reached a high pitch of civilization. We are therefore dealing not with exceptional facts, which might justifiably be overlooked, but with a general and, in the widest sense of the word, a human phenomenon, the kind of phenomenon which cannot be disregarded by anyone who is trying to discover what religion is, and what are the deep needs which it must satisfy."

Ideally, everyone should be able to find self-transcendence in some form of pure or applied religion. In practice it seems very unlikely that this hoped for consummation will ever be realized. There are, and doubtless there always will be, good churchmen and good churchwomen for whom, unfortunately, piety is not enough. The late G. K. Chesterton, who wrote at least as lyrically of drink as of devotion, may serve as their eloquent spokesman.

The modern churches, with some exceptions among the Protestant denominations, tolerate alcohol; but even the most tolerant have made no attempt to convert the drug to Christianity, or to sacramentalize its use. The pious drinker is forced to take his religion in one compartment, his religion-surrogate in another. And perhaps this is inevitable. Drinking cannot be sacramentalized except in religions which set no store on decorum. The worship of Dionysos or the Celtic god of beer was a loud and disorderly affair. The rites of Christianity are incompatible with even religious drunkenness. This does no harm to the distillers, but is very bad for Christianity. Countless persons desire self-transcendence and would be glad to find it in church. But, alas, "the hungry sheep look up and are not fed." They take part in rites, they listen to sermons, they repeat prayers; but their thirst remains unassuaged. Disappointed, they turn to the bottle. For a time at least and in a kind of way, it works. Church may still be attended; but it is no more than the Musical Bank of Butler's *Erewhon*. God may still be acknowledged; but He is God only on the verbal level, only in a strictly Pickwickian sense. The effective object of worship is the bottle and the sole religious experience is that state of uninhibited and belligerent euphoria which follows the ingestion of the third cocktail.

We see, then, that Christianity and alcohol do not and cannot mix. Christianity and mescalin seem to be much more compatible. This has been demonstrated by many tribes of Indians, from Texas to as far north as Wisconsin. Among these tribes are to be found groups affiliated with the Native American Church, a sect whose principal rite is a kind of Early Christian agape, or love feast, where slices of peyote take the place of the sacramental bread and wine. These Native Americans regard the cactus as God's special gift to the Indians, and equate its effects with the workings of the divine Spirit.

Professor J. S. Slotkin, one of the very few white men ever to have participated in the rites of a Peyotist congregation, says of his fellow worshipers that they are "certainly not stupefied or drunk. . . . They never get out of rhythm or fumble their words, as a drunken or stupefied man would do. . . . They are all quiet, courteous and considerate of one another. I have never been in any white man's house of worship where there is either so much religious feeling or decorum." And what, we may ask, are these devout and well-behaved Peyotists experiencing? Not the mild sense of virtue which sustains the average Sunday churchgoer through ninety minutes of boredom. Not even those high feelings, inspired by thoughts of the Creator and the Redeemer, the Judge and the Comforter, which animate the pious. For these Native Americans, religious experience is something more direct and illuminating, more spontaneous, less the homemade product of the superficial, self-conscious mind. Sometimes (according to the reports collected by Dr. Slotkin) they see visions, which may be of Christ Himself. Sometimes they hear the voice of the Great Spirit. Sometimes they become aware of the presence of God and of those personal shortcomings which must be corrected if they are to do His will. The practical consequences of these chemical openings of doors into the Other World seem to be wholly good. Dr. Slotkin reports that habitual Peyotists are on the whole more industrious, more temperate (many of them abstain altogether from alcohol), more peaceable than non-Peyotists. A tree with such satisfactory fruits cannot be condemned out of hand as evil.

In sacramentalizing the use of peyote, the Indians of the Native American Church have done something which is at once psychologically sound and historically respectable. In the early centuries of Christianity many pagan rites and festivals were baptized, so to say, and made to serve the purposes of the Church. These jollifications were not particularly edifying; but they assuaged a certain psychological hunger and, instead of trying to suppress them, the earlier missionaries had the sense to accept them for what they were, soul-satisfying expressions of fundamental urges, and to incorporate them into the fabric of the new religion. What the Native Americans have done is essentially similar. They have taken a pagan custom (a custom, incidentally, far more elevating and enlightening than most of the rather brutish carousals and mummeries adopted from European paganism) and given it a Christian significance.

Though but recently introduced into the northern United States, peyote-eating and the religion based upon it have become important symbols of the red man's right to spiritual independence. Some Indians have reacted to white supremacy by becoming Americanized, others by retreating into traditional Indianism. But some have tried to make the best of both worlds, indeed of all the worlds—the best of Indianism, the best of Christianity, and the best of those Other Worlds of transcendental experience, where the soul knows itself as unconditioned and of like nature with the divine. Hence the Native American Church. In it two great appetites of the soul— the urge to independence and self-determination and the urge to self-transcendence—were fused with, and interpreted in the light of, a third—the urge to worship, to justify the ways of God to man, to explain the universe by means of a coherent theology.

> Lo, the poor Indian, whose untutored mind
> Clothes him in front, but leaves him bare behind.

But actually it is we, the rich and highly educated whites, who have left ourselves bare behind. We cover our anterior nakedness with some philosophy—Christian, Marxian, Freudo-Physicalist—but abaft we remain uncovered, at the mercy of all the winds of circumstance. The poor Indian, on the other hand, has had the wit to protect his rear by supplementing the fig leaf of a theology with the breechclout of transcendental experience.

I am not so foolish as to equate what happens under the influence of mescalin or of any other drug, prepared or in the future preparable, with the realization of the end and ultimate purpose of human life: Enlightenment, the Beatific Vision. All I am suggesting is that the mescalin experience is what Catholic theologians call "a gratuitous grace," not necessary to salvation but potentially helpful and to be accepted thankfully, if made available. To be shaken out of the ruts of ordinary perception, to be shown for a few timeless hours the outer and the inner world, not as they appear to an animal obsessed with survival or to a human being obsessed with words and notions, but as they are apprehended, directly and unconditionally, by Mind at Large—this is an experience of inestimable value to everyone and especially to the intellectual. For the intellectual is by definition the man for whom, in Goethe's phrase, "the word is essentially fruitful." He is the man who feels that "what we perceive by the eye is foreign to us as such and need not impress us deeply." And yet, though himself an intellectual and one of the supreme masters of language, Goethe did not always agree with his own evaluation of the word. "We talk," he wrote in middle life, "far too much. We should talk less and draw more. I personally should like to renounce speech altogether and, like organic Nature, communicate everything I have to say in sketches. That fig tree, this little snake, the cocoon on my window sill quietly awaiting its future—all these are momentous signatures. A person able to decipher their meaning properly would soon be able to dispense with the written or the spoken word altogether. The more I think of it, there is something futile, mediocre, even (I am tempted to say) foppish about speech. By contrast, how the gravity of Nature and her silence startle you, when you stand face to face with her, undistracted, before a barren ridge or in the desolation of the ancient hills." We can never dispense with language and the other symbol systems; for it is by means of them, and only by their means, that we have raised ourselves above the brutes, to the level of human beings. But we can easily become the victims as well as the beneficiaries of these systems. We must learn how to handle words effectively; but at the same time we must preserve and, if necessary, intensify our ability to look at the world directly and not through that half opaque medium of concepts, which distorts every given fact into the all too familiar likeness of some generic label or explanatory abstraction.

Literary or scientific, liberal or specialist, all our education is predominantly verbal and therefore fails to accomplish what it is supposed to do. Instead of transforming children into fully developed adults, it turns out students of the natural sciences who are completely unaware of Nature as the primary fact of experience, it inflicts upon the world students of the humanities who know nothing of humanity, their own or anyone else's.

Gestalt psychologists, such as Samuel Renshaw, have devised methods for widening the range and increasing the acuity of human perceptions. But do our educators apply them? The answer is, No.

Teachers in every field of psycho-physical skill, from seeing to tennis, from tightrope walking to prayer, have discovered, by trial and error, the conditions of optimum functioning within their special fields. But have any of the great Foundations financed a project for co-ordinating these empirical findings into a general theory and practice of heightened creativeness? Again, so far as I am aware, the answer is, No.

All sorts of cultists and queer fish teach all kinds of techniques for achieving health, contentment, peace of mind; and for many of their hearers many of these techniques are demonstrably effective. But do we see respectable psychologists, philosophers and clergymen boldly descending into those odd and sometimes malodorous wells, at the bottom of which poor Truth is so often condemned to sit? Yet once more the answer is, No.

And now look at the history of mescalin research. Seventy years ago men of first-rate ability described the transcendental experiences which come to those who, in good health, under proper conditions and in the right spirit, take the drug. How many philosophers, how many theologians, how many professional educators have had the curiosity to open this Door in the Wall? The answer, for all practical purposes, is, None.

In a world where education is predominantly verbal, highly educated people find it all but impossible to pay serious attention to anything but words and notions. There is always money for, there are always doctorates in, the learned foolery of research into what, for scholars, is the all-important problem: Who influenced whom to say what when? Even in this age of technology the verbal humanities are honored. The non-verbal humanities, the arts of being directly aware of the given facts of our existence, are almost completely ignored. A catalogue, a bibliography, a definitive edition of a third-rate versifier's *ipsissima verba,* a stupendous index to end all indexes—any genuinely Alexandrian project is sure of approval and financial support. But when it comes to finding out how you and I, our children and grandchildren, may become more perceptive, more intensely aware of inward and outward reality, more open to the Spirit, less apt, by psychological malpractices, to make ourselves physically ill, and more capable of controlling our own autonomic nervous system—when it comes to any form of non-verbal education more fundamental (and more likely to be of some practical use) than Swedish drill, no really respectable person in any really respectable university or church will do anything about it. Verbalists are suspicious of the non-verbal; rationalists fear the given, non-rational fact; intellectuals feel that "what we perceive by the eye (or in any other way) is foreign to us as such and need not impress us deeply." Besides, this matter of education in the non-verbal humanities will not fit into any of the established pigeon-holes. It is not religion, not neurology, not gymnastics, not morality or civics, not even experimental psychology. This being so the subject is, for academic and ecclesiastical purposes, non-existent and may safely be ignored altogether or left, with a patronizing smile, to those whom the Pharisees of verbal orthodoxy call cranks, quacks, charlatans and unqualified amateurs.

"I have always found," Blake wrote rather bitterly, "that Angels have the vanity to speak of themselves as the only wise. This they do with a confident insolence sprouting from systematic reasoning."

Systematic reasoning is something we could not, as a species or as individuals, possibly do without. But neither, if we are to remain sane, can we possibly do without direct perception, the more unsystematic the better, of the inner and outer worlds into which we have been born. This given reality is an infinite which passes all understanding and yet admits of being directly and in some sort totally apprehended. It is a transcendence belonging to another order than the human, and yet it may be present to us as a felt immanence, an experienced participation. To be enlightened is to be aware, always, of total reality in its immanent otherness—to be aware of it and yet to remain in a condition to survive as an animal, to think and feel as a human being, to resort whenever expedient to systematic reasoning. Our goal is to discover that we have always been where we ought to be. Unhappily we make the task exceedingly difficult for ourselves. Meanwhile, however, there are gratuitous graces in the form of partial and fleeting realizations. Under a more realistic, a less exclusively verbal system of education than ours, every Angel (in Blake's sense of that word) would be permitted as a sabbatical treat, would be urged and even, if necessary, compelled to take an occasional trip through some chemical Door in the Wall into the world of transcendental experience. If it terrified him, it would be unfortunate but probably salutary. If it brought him a brief but timeless illumination, so much the better. In either case the Angel might lose a little of the confident insolence sprouting from systematic reasoning and the consciousness of having read all the books.

Near the end of his life Aquinas experienced Infused Contemplation. Thereafter he refused to go back to work on his unfinished book. Compared with *this*, everything he had read and argued about and written—Aristotle and the Sentences, the Questions, the Propositions, the majestic Summas—was no better than chaff or straw. For most intellectuals such a sit-down strike would be inadvisable, even morally wrong. But the Angelic Doctor had done more systematic reasoning than any twelve ordinary Angels, and was already ripe for death. He had earned the right, in those last months of his mortality, to turn away from merely symbolic straw and chaff to the bread of actual and substantial Fact. For Angels of a lower order and with better prospects of longevity, there must be a return to the straw. But the man who comes back through the Door in the Wall will never be quite the same as the man who went out. He will be wiser but less cocksure, happier but less self-satisfied, humbler in acknowledging his ignorance yet better equipped to understand the relationship of words to things, of systematic reasoning to the unfathomable Mystery which it tries, forever vainly, to comprehend.